ROCKSTAR REVENUE

BJÖRGVIN BENEDIKTSSON

ROCKSTAR REVENUE

EARN MORE FROM YOUR CREATIVE SKILLS

(WITHOUT FEELING LIKE A SELLOUT)

*For Liz, the real rockstar CEO of our family,
and her two groupies, Lilja Sif and Matti Ben.*

FREE GIFT

As a way of saying thank you for your purchase I want to give you exclusive access to the Rockstar Revenue bonus bundle from my website.

- **Business Launch Checklist - Your Step-by-Step Start-up Plan (Without the Headache):** Never started a business before? No problem. This simple checklist outlines everything you need to turn your business from idea to registered in your area, ready to sell to customers. No fluff. No legalese. Just the steps you need to go pro without losing your mind.

- **Go-To-Market Blueprint - Define Your Audience, Dial In Your Message, and Create Stuff People Actually Want:** If you've ever stared at a blank screen wondering who you're even making this for—this one's for you. This fill-in-the-blank workbook helps you identify your dream clients, clarify your offer, and test it fast (before you build a thing). Skip the overwhelm. Define your audience, message, and offer so you have a clear roadmap of what to do, and when to do it.

- **Creative's Pricing Calculator - Charge What You're Worth Without Guessing or Cringing:** This plug-and-play calculator helps you figure out what to charge for your products or services—based on actual numbers, not vibes. Whether you're pricing a course, a sample pack, or a mixing job, this tool has your back. Knowing your numbers is everything. This calculator crunches the numbers for you, making it easy to know what to charge to maximize profit and shrink the timeline to your financial goals.

These high-value, high-impact bonus bundle is available to you for absolutely free for being a Rockstar Revenue reader. Simply go to www.bbenediktsson.com/rockstar-bonuses to claim your free bonus bundle.

Enjoy!

Björgvin

TABLE OF CONTENTS

INTRODUCTION
WHY THIS BOOK MATTERS

I met Laura years ago when she was on a musicians' panel at the TENWEST conference in Tucson. The panel discussed touring, releasing records, and working as an indie musician, drawing on their varied experiences to offer the audience insightful nuggets of wisdom, coupled with crazy stories from the road. I didn't know Laura that well, but we were part of the same music scene, so there was a common understanding of the fun and frustration that came with being an indie musician.

Afterwards, a few of us from the conference gathered at a nearby bar to chat, and we began discussing her band. It turned out that she wanted to go back on tour to promote her new album, but her bass player had quit the band. He didn't want to be on the road any longer because he wanted to spend time with his family. Hacking it on the road as an independent touring musician wasn't worth it to him with kids at home, so Laura was stuck.

So I lied to her.

I told her, "Sure, I can play bass. I've got a flexible schedule. I can go on tour."

Only two of those things were true, but as a guitar player, I thought, "how hard could it be? There's only four strings!"

Luckily for me, Laura and the Killed Men, as she called us, was an Americana band, so the bass playing was fairly straightforward. The outgoing bass player was gracious enough to teach me all their songs and after a few weeks of rehearsal, we were ready for our Southwest tour.

We traveled all the way north up to San Francisco and as east as Austin, and let me tell you: there's no better place to hone your chops than onstage in front of a live audience. Playing in public will improve your skills exponentially faster than if you give yourself the luxury of practicing alone.

Sidenote: There's a lesson there about creating minimum viable products and launching products before you're ready, but that's a lesson for another time.

During the tour, a band from Alaska invited us to join them for a few shows in the Last Frontier. Since they had connections with venues up north, we decided (on nothing but a wish and a prayer) to expand those shows into a month-long Alaskan tour. While we were working our way back to Arizona, on the 8-hour stretch from Amarillo, TX, to Flagstaff, AZ, we booked our flights.

That summer, we landed in Anchorage and performed all over the state for about a month.

Once the month was over, we tallied our performance revenue, deducted our costs, and realized we made....$1,000. Split four ways. For a month's worth of work.

That last week of tour, I also ran my regular Audio Issues summer sale, and in the 24 hours before we counted our indie music money, my business had made that AND some. Split one way. For products I had made years before, and a few emails that took thirty minutes to write.

That's the power of "Auto-Pilot Products" for you, and I wrote this book so that you can experience all that your creative career has to offer. I want you to feel secure that you know how to make money *when you need it*, even if you want to run off and join the circus, or, like me, tour with an indie band.

Sleeping on the floors and couches of random strangers and making less than minimum wage performing at random bars and clubs around the country might not be the most glamorous lifestyle in the world, but I'm glad that I did it. Especially because I had my little online business chugging along on the side, making sure I was taken care of while I enjoyed the life of a wannabe rockstar.

FINDING MY FREQUENCY: HOW I TURNED MY PASSION FOR AUDIO INTO A CAREER

I didn't start as an expert in the audio industry.

My first job in live sound was a chaotic mess of twisting knobs, hoping I was doing something right, and figuring things out on the fly. The hours were long, the pay was low, but the thrill of working in audio–the pure energy of working with bands on stage and making them sound good–had me hooked.

Somewhere in that whirlwind, I found my passion. I loved audio so much that my bosses at the time recognized that passion and encouraged me to pursue it. So I enrolled in an audio engineering program at the SAE Institute. SAE has campuses all over the world, but I decided to join the one in Madrid, Spain, to learn Spanish at the same time.

But life, as it often does, threw me a curveball.

In 2008, at the height of the recession, I lost all my savings. Everything I had worked for was gone in an instant. However, I was fortunate enough to have already paid for my tuition before the crash. That meant I could still follow through with my plans and study audio engineering in Spain at the SAE Institute. It was a gamble, but one that would ultimately change my life.

That's where my brand, **Audio Issues,** was born. Not as a business, not as a brand, but as an idea. At first, I wasn't even teaching. I was just writing. Writing down everything I was learning on a little blog I had recently started, hoping to make sense of it and maybe even help someone else who was trying to navigate the confusing world of audio.

Whenever I'm asked about my "success" I always tell them this story. I simply started writing down what I was learning and what I knew. And then I never really stopped. The more I wrote, the bigger my audience became. These simple blog posts attracted a growing audience, and before I knew it, **Audio Issues** had taken on a life of its own.

Over the years—nearly 20 now—I've done live sound, broadcast radio recording, and studio mixing. I've been a touring musician. I've worked at music festivals like Bonnaroo, where I've recorded big-name bands such as Walk the Moon, Sheryl Crow, and Alt-J, among many others. I've done radio recordings with some incredible artists like Andrew Bird. And I've also released records as an indie musician, both in the band The Long Wait, and more recently as the solo artist, Random Somebody. Because if this random somebody can release their art into the world, so can you.

Additionally, I've spent years sharing my knowledge, writing for prominent publications such as **MusicTech Magazine** and **The Recording Revolution,** and contributing to industry podcasts like **Recording Studio Rockstars**.

I've been creating content for almost 20 years now, and this book is just one more piece of content I love sharing with the world.

Over time, I transformed my knowledge into digital products, including books, courses, templates, and software, which not only generated an income but also did so on autopilot.

At the heart of it all, I'm still doing what I started—learning, creating, and paying it forward. Because if there's one thing I've learned in this journey, it's that **knowledge grows when you share it**. And that's exactly why I do what I do.

Today, my online business, Audio Issues, has helped thousands of musicians and producers create professional-quality music from the comfort of their own home studios.

My business now runs largely without my constant involvement, giving me the flexibility to pursue other ventures, including mentoring entrepreneurs and advising startups.

This book is my way of paying forward the lessons I've learned.

I'm glad you're here, and I hope this gives you a little insight into where I'm coming from.

Björgvin Benediktsson
May, 2025

STOP TRADING TIME FOR MONEY

Many freelancers and service providers get stuck in a cycle of trading time for money. This model can be rewarding, but it's also exhausting and limits your earning potential. If you don't work, you don't get paid. That's where product-based businesses come in.

By creating digital products—such as books, courses, templates, and software—you can generate income repeatedly from a single piece of work. Instead of constantly hunting for new clients, your products work for you, even while you sleep. This approach allows you to:

- Earn passive income without constantly selling your time.
- Reach a global audience without geographical limitations.
- Scale your earnings beyond what's possible with one-on-one services.

Both are valid options, but if you want freedom, flexibility, and a way to scale beyond your own time, a product-based business is crucial. That's what this book is about.

I'm living proof that this model works. Like I've mentioned before, if a random somebody from a small town in Iceland can build a six-figure online business, so can you.

WHY PRODUCT-BASED BUSINESSES OFFER FINANCIAL FREEDOM

How are you going to break through the six-figure mark if you're stuck trading time for money?

Let's break it down with some simple math. The average person working a full-time job—40 hours a week—logs about 2,080 hours per year. To hit six figures, you'd need to charge at least $48 to $50 per hour. But here's the catch: That assumes you're billing for every single one of those hours.

In reality, that's just not how business works.

Even if you're a highly skilled freelancer, consultant, or service provider, you're not spending the full 40 hours every week doing paid client work. Some of your time is spent on marketing, networking, sending invoices, maintaining your website, and improving your skills. Not to mention administrative work, responding to emails, or just taking a break. The idea that you can sustain a perfect 40-hour billable workweek is unrealistic.

And that's where the income ceiling kicks in.

If you're solely relying on billable hours, you're essentially stuck in a time-for-money trap. There's only so much time in a day, and once your calendar is full, your income is capped, *unless* you raise your rates.

However, even then, there is a limit to what clients are willing to pay, and constantly increasing prices isn't a scalable long-term strategy.

So, how do you break past that income ceiling?

The answer lies in creating products that generate revenue without requiring you to trade more time.

This is where **autopilot products** come in: digital courses, e-books, subscription services, membership sites, templates, or even software. These types of products enable you to earn money while you sleep, work on other projects, or even while taking time off.

Think about it: If you create a course that teaches people what you already know—something you're constantly explaining to clients—you only have to build it once. After that, it can be sold an unlimited number of times, with little to no extra effort on your part. That's how you scale.

Instead of working 40+ hours a week trying to maximize billable hours, you shift toward building something that pays you repeatedly.

The most successful entrepreneurs don't just trade time for money. They create leverage. And that leverage comes from autopilot products that free them from the constant hustle of hourly work.

So if you want to break through six figures and beyond, it's time to start thinking about how to make your knowledge, skills, and expertise work for you, even when you're not actively working.

THE IMPORTANCE OF DIVERSIFIED INCOME

A diversified income strategy means you're not reliant on a single client, employer, or business model. Instead, you spread your earnings across multiple channels, such as:

- **Digital products:** Books, courses, templates, and memberships.
- **Affiliate marketing:** Earning commissions by promoting other products.
- **Consulting or coaching:** High-ticket services that complement your passive income.
- **Advertising and sponsorships:** Monetizing your platform through partnerships.

This book will guide you through building your own diversified income streams, giving you more financial stability and freedom.

By the end of this book, you'll have a clear roadmap to creating a profitable online business that allows you to work smarter, not harder.

Let's get started!

CHAPTER 1
WHO DO YOU NEED TO BECOME?

When I started out, I was just some kid from a small town in Iceland, twisting knobs at live gigs, trying to figure out how audio worked.

I had no business experience, no marketing background. I just had a passion for music and an obsession with figuring things out. I had no idea that the skills I was learning would one day evolve into a full-fledged online business serving thousands of customers all over the world. But looking back, every step of the journey led me here.

Fast forward to today, and I've built a six-figure business helping musicians release radio-ready music, launched multiple successful products, and even started mentoring other entrepreneurs.

Here's the kicker: I didn't start out as the person who could do all of this. I became that person by showing up daily, learning, adapting, and pushing forward, even when I had no idea what I was doing.

And that's what you need to do too. You don't need to be an expert right now. You just need to be willing to learn, experiment, and grow into the person who runs a successful product-based business.

Your business is an extension of you. It evolves as you grow. The skills you develop, the experiences you gain, and the challenges you overcome all contribute to what you can offer. You don't need to have it all figured out from day one. Start where you are, learn along the way, and build something that fits your strengths and passions.

OVERCOMING SELF-DOUBT

If you've ever thought, *"Who am I to teach this?"* or *"What if nobody buys what I create?"*, you're not alone. Every creative entrepreneur faces self-doubt at some point. The trick is to push through it.

If you've done something successfully—even just for yourself—you have enough experience to help someone else. You don't need a degree, a certification, or 10 years of experience. You just need to know how to get from point A to point B and be able to teach someone else to do the same.

I didn't start with a huge audience. I started by sharing what I was learning, and over time, people began to pay attention. You don't have to be the world's greatest expert. You just need to be a few steps ahead of the people you're helping. Your knowledge and experience are valuable, even if they seem basic to you.

One way to overcome self-doubt is to focus on results. If you've achieved something—no matter how small—you can help others do the same. Teach what you know, document your journey, and refine your process as you go. Confidence comes from taking action, not waiting until you feel ready.

Think about it: I built a business teaching people how to mix music. Not because I had a Grammy, but because I figured out a process that worked and shared it with others. That's it.

So if you've been holding back because you feel like you're not "ready," stop. You'll never feel 100% ready. Just start.

OVERCOMING CHALLENGES AND STAYING MOTIVATED

Building a successful autopilot business is exciting, but it comes with its own set of challenges. The key to long-term success is persistence, adaptability, and staying motivated even when things get tough. Here are a few common challenges and how you can overcome them.

1. IMPOSTER SYNDROME

- Feeling like you're not qualified to teach or sell? Well, I'm sure half your high-school teachers were only a step or two ahead of you, and that's all you need to help others too.
- Focus on the results you've achieved and how you can help others achieve the same success.

2. LACK OF IMMEDIATE RESULTS

- Autopilot products take time to gain traction.
- Like I'll show you later on in this book, it doesn't have to take you longer than three weeks to see results. But remember, consistency is key.

3. TECHNICAL OVERWHELM

- You don't need to master every tool. Start with simple platforms and scale up from there.
- If you can share your knowledge on Zoom, put together a few slides and screenshare, you can make a simple product that sells.

4. BURNOUT AND LOSING MOTIVATION

- Set realistic goals and celebrate small wins.
- Take breaks and allow yourself creative downtime.

THE POWER OF MINDSET

Success in business is just as much about mindset as it is about marketing strategy. Stay committed to learning, growing, and adapting. Surround yourself with supportive peers and mentors who can encourage you through the tough moments.

DEFINING SUCCESS ON YOUR TERMS

Success isn't about hitting a specific revenue number or gaining thousands of followers. It's about designing a business that supports the life you want to live.

For me, success meant freedom—freedom to work on projects I love, spend time with my family, and travel without worrying about where my next paycheck would come from. Your version of success might be different. Maybe it's earning enough to quit your job, or having more time to create without financial stress.

Take a moment to define what success looks like for you. When you have a clear vision, it's easier to stay motivated and focused on building a business that truly aligns with your goals.

THE FOUR QUESTIONS YOU NEED TO ASK YOURSELF BEFORE BUILDING ANYTHING

Before you start building a business, a product, or even a new offer, there are four essential questions you need to ask yourself. These questions will save you time, effort, and frustration by ensuring that what you're creating is both viable and worth committing to in the long run.

But first, a word of caution: **Don't take advice from people who haven't actually done what they're telling you to do.**

If someone is giving you business advice but has never built a business themselves, take that with a grain of salt. Real experience matters. Learn from those who have successfully done what you want to do, not just those who talk about it.

Now, let's dive into the four key questions.

1. ARE YOU QUALIFIED TO HELP PEOPLE GET FROM A TO B?

The first thing I want to make sure you do is **ask yourself whether you're actually qualified to help others achieve a specific result.** Have you successfully done it yourself? And more importantly, can you do it consistently?

Because **if you know exactly how to do something consistently, it's easily replicable, and you can create a system around it**—one that you can sell.

This has nothing to do with being famous, award-winning, or having some high-profile industry title. External validation doesn't matter here. What matters is whether you can reliably **deliver a result, over and over again.**

For example, take one of my Auto-Pilot Products students. Kenneth is an accomplished bass player. He knows how to play bass, and more importantly, he can play bass **consistently.** He's not a terrible bass player one day and an amazing one the next. He possesses a repeatable skill set, which means he can effectively teach others.

Teaching is a separate skill, of course, but it's much easier to teach something when you actually **know how to do it** rather than just theorizing about it. People don't need vague, hypothetical advice. They need clear, actionable steps that help them get results. And you can only provide that if you have real-world experience.

2. IS THERE A MARKET FOR IT?

Passion is great, but if no one is willing to pay for what you're offering, it's not a business—it's a hobby.

You need to make sure there's a **hungry market** of people who need what you offer and are willing to pay for it.

The easiest way to validate this? **Check for competition.**

If there are already people selling products or services in the space you want to enter, that's actually a **good** sign. It means there's demand.

Take the audio industry, for example. There are numerous websites, courses, and products available that teach audio engineering and mixing. That tells me there's a **real market** for this kind of education. **Audio Issues** is just one piece of that much larger market.

If nobody is selling anything in the space you're interested in, that's **not** a good sign. It usually doesn't mean you've discovered an untapped opportunity. It probably means there's no demand.

At the same time, there's another extreme: **oversaturation.** If an industry is completely flooded, and everyone is racing to the bottom by offering everything for free or at deep discounts, then it becomes difficult to command real value.

For example, in some areas of online education, there's been a rush to give away information for free. If you enter a market like that, you'll struggle to sell because people have been conditioned to expect things at rock-bottom prices.

You need to find a balance. A market that has demand but where you can still differentiate yourself and charge what you're worth.

3. CAN YOU STAND OUT IN THIS MARKET?

If there's competition, you need to find a way to **differentiate yourself.**

This doesn't mean reinventing the wheel. It just means carving out a unique position for yourself. Maybe you focus on a specific audience, a particular way of teaching, or a different kind of content delivery.

Ask yourself:

- What makes my approach to this unique?
- What specific audience am I serving?
- How can I position my product or service in a way that resonates with people differently than what's already out there?

For example, in the world of audio education, there are many different approaches—some focus on high-end studio techniques, others cater to bedroom producers, and some teach in-depth music theory alongside production.

My approach with **Audio Issues** has always been practical and accessible, helping people make professional-sounding mixes without getting lost in technical jargon. I make the audio jargon easy to understand so that you can focus on making music without getting stuck in the engineering. That's my unique angle.

You don't have to be **the** best. You just have to be the best fit for **your** audience.

4. DO YOU ACTUALLY WANT TO DO THIS?

This is the most important question of all.

We're not just doing this for a few weeks or months. I hope you're committing to **years** of building and growing. I've been at this for over **15 years** now, and I wouldn't have stuck with it through the ups and downs if I didn't genuinely enjoy it.

Ask yourself: **Do you truly want to pursue this in the long term?**

Because if you don't, it will feel like a chore. And if your business feels like a job you hate, what's the point? The whole idea is to build something that's **enjoyable** to work on—even when things aren't going well.

I love creating products.

I love teaching.

I love packaging knowledge in a way that helps people.

Even when I launch a product that doesn't do as well as I hoped, I still learn something from it. Sure, it's discouraging in the moment, but I enjoy the process enough to **keep going.** That's what keeps me in the game.

And here's the reality: **It will take longer than you think, and it will be harder than you expect.**

If you're only in it for the money, you'll burn out fast. But if you genuinely enjoy the work, you'll push through the tough times, learn from your failures, and keep improving.

FINAL THOUGHTS

Before you commit to building something, take a step back and ask yourself:

Am I truly qualified to help people with this?

Is there an actual market willing to pay for it?

Do I have a way to stand out in that market?

Do I genuinely want to dedicate years to this?

If you can confidently answer **yes** to all four, you're in a great position to build something meaningful and sustainable. If not, take the time to refine your idea, conduct further research, or explore something else that aligns better with your skills, the market, and your long-term objectives.

Success isn't just about having a good idea. It's about building something that lasts. And that starts by asking the right questions before you begin.

THE 4P FRAMEWORK

PERSON + PLATFORM + PRODUCT = PROFIT

Success with an Auto-Pilot Product isn't random. It's built on a strong foundation of strategy. That's where the **4P Framework** comes in. This model ensures that you're set up for sustainable growth by focusing on four essential pillars:

- **Person**
- **Platform**
- **Product**
- **and Profit**

PERSON (OR WHO DO YOU NEED TO BE TO SUCCEED?)

Getting clarity on the people you wish to serve so that your message resonates with your customers is a crucial part of building your business. But more importantly, so is figuring out the person you need to become in order to serve your customers at the highest level.

Before you can build a thriving autopilot business, you need to develop the right mindset and skill set. Ask yourself:

- What expertise do I already have that others might find valuable?
- What topics am I passionate about that I could create content or products around?

- How do I want to show up in my business—teacher, coach, creator, or mentor?

You don't have to be the world's top expert, but you do need to know your craft well enough to help others succeed. The goal is to leverage your knowledge and experience to create value for your audience.

CHOOSING THE RIGHT PLATFORM

Optimizing your online platform and systemizing your marketing systems is key to avoiding overwhelm. Automation through software and outsourced service providers means that you spend less time working in your business and more time being creative.

Your platform is where people find you, consume your content, and eventually become customers. There are different types of platforms you can build your brand on:

- **Owned Platforms** (Your website, email list, private community)
- **Social Media** (YouTube, Instagram, LinkedIn, Twitter, TikTok)
- **Content Platforms** (Podcasting, blogging, online courses)

The best approach? Start with one owned platform, and one social channel to master. Then grow from there. You don't need to be everywhere at once. Focus on where your audience spends the most time.

CREATING A PRODUCT THAT ALIGNS WITH YOUR STRENGTHS

Once you have clarity on who you serve and where they find you, the next step is product creation. Creating digital products and creating diversified passive income streams enables you to free up your time and earn more money without spending more time working.

Your product should:

- Solve a specific problem.
- Be easy for your audience to consume and implement.
- Align with your natural strengths—whether that's writing, teaching, or designing.

Some common autopilot product ideas include:

- **E-books & Guides:** A simple and effective way to package your knowledge.
- **Online Courses:** A structured learning experience that helps customers achieve results.
- **Templates & Toolkits:** Pre-made resources that save people time and effort.
- **Memberships & Subscriptions:** Ongoing value that generates recurring revenue.

HOW TO FIGURE OUT WHAT PRODUCTS YOU CAN CREATE

If you're wondering what kind of products you can create, here are some questions to help point you in the right direction.

- What skills have you developed?
- What do people ask for your advice on?
- What do you get questions about from friends, family, or colleagues?
- What are you really good at or an expert in?
- What would you do in your free time that people don't know how to do?
- What's easy for you that's hard for others?
- What challenges have you overcome?

Let's go through these questions and I'll also give you some examples from my own experience.

WHAT SKILLS HAVE YOU DEVELOPED?

How do you filter out what's worth pursuing? Here's a simple exercise:

Make a list of all the skills, hobbies, and experiences you have. Be comprehensive—write down everything, even the things that seem insignificant.

Identify the skills that others struggle with. What comes easily to you that others find difficult?

Consider what people are already asking you for help with. If you keep getting the same questions, there's a demand for your knowledge.

Think about what you love doing in your free time that others would pay for. This is where passion meets profitability.

Obviously, **audio engineering** is a major skill of mine—I built **Audio Issues** based on that. But after marketing my products and running an online business for so long, people started asking me for advice on that too.

There's an entire segment of people who want to know:

- How do you build these kinds of products?
- How do you come up with content?
- How do you run an online business?

So that's why I'm here, doing this. Because I get these questions all the time. And by putting this information out there, my goal is to help others do the same. Because if I can do it, **so can you.**

WHAT ARE YOU REALLY GOOD AT OR AN EXPERT IN?

I'm good at a lot of different things—but not all of them are worth turning into a business.

For example, I really enjoy **cooking** and I think I'm pretty good at it. But I'm not going to start a recipe blog. I'm not going to launch a restaurant. Sounds like a terrible lifestyle for me so I'm going to avoid that like the plague, thank you very much.

Why do I have such strong feelings about that? Well...I actually did have a small business in the food space for a while. I used to sell cookie mixes, but I hated the work. It became a job I despised, something I dreaded doing every day. I had to make 300 cookie samples every Friday for the Farmer's Markets over the weekend and then I spent the entire weekend standing at a stall slinging cookies.

Don't get me wrong, I'd sell hundreds of cookie mixes each time. My sales spiel converted like crazy and I sold hundreds of dollars worth of cookies every weekend. But, it also meant that my weekends were never free.

And most importantly, it took away time I wanted to spend with my young daughter. I didn't want to miss her first few years growing up just to sell people some cookie mixes. So just because you're good at something doesn't mean it's the right fit for a business OR your lifestyle.

So make a list of all the things you're good at, then narrow it down. Pick the ones that feel the most desirable to you **and** make sense from a market perspective.

WHAT WOULD YOU DO IN YOUR FREE TIME THAT PEOPLE DON'T KNOW HOW TO DO?

This is where you find the intersection between **a hobby and something people will pay for.**

For me, obviously, any **music-related** skills fit here: playing guitar, playing bass, writing songs. Even things like **journaling, writing poetry, or storytelling** fit in this category.

WHAT'S EASY FOR YOU THAT'S HARD FOR OTHERS?

This is just another way of framing the previous question, but it's important to think about.

Maybe you're a really great poet or short story writer, and it comes naturally to you—which, by the way, I'd be very jealous of if that's the case. But that could be something you enjoy teaching other people, because it's easy for you but hard for others.

What do you do effortlessly that other people struggle with? That's where real business potential is—because people are willing to pay for expertise that saves them **time, frustration, or mistakes.**

WHAT CHALLENGES HAVE YOU OVERCOME?

This one is huge. Because the best businesses are often built around solving a challenge that you've personally dealt with and now know how to navigate.

Sometimes, the most valuable business ideas don't come from what you're good at, but from what you've struggled with and conquered.

For example, I'm Icelandic, but I'm now an American citizen. I naturalized in 2020, and then, of course, the world promptly ended. I really hope my naturalization didn't cause COVID, but those two things *did* happen within a very short time.

Going through that process: getting a green card, legally immigrating, and naturalizing was incredibly challenging. It required an **insane** amount of paperwork.

Now, could I turn around and start a business helping people move from an F1 visa to a green card, or teaching them how to become U.S. citizens? **Yes.**

Do I want to do that? **Hell no.**

I never want to see that paperwork again. But it's still an example of a **huge** challenge that I could theoretically help people with if I wanted to.

For you, maybe there's a challenge you've overcome that you'd actually **love** helping people through.

Another personal example: I've been **alcohol-free for two years.** That's something I'm really proud of, but I don't talk about it too much, though I guess I am now, writing this for everyone to read.

There are plenty of people who have built entire brands around **sobriety, addiction recovery, and alcohol-free living.** And that's awesome. But for me, it's just a personal journey. I love connecting with others who have been through it, but I **don't** want to build a business around it.

That's important to recognize: **Just because you've overcome something doesn't mean you have to turn it into a brand.** But if you're passionate about it and enjoy helping people through it, it could be a great foundation for a business.

The point is, you have **unique experiences and challenges that others are going through right now.** If you've overcome something significant, you could help others do the same—and that's the foundation of a powerful business.

YOUR TURN: BRAINSTORM YOUR BUSINESS IDEAS

Now it's your turn.

Take **five minutes** to brainstorm answers to these questions:

- What skills have you developed?
- What do people naturally ask you for advice on?
- What are you really good at?
- What would you do in your free time that others don't know how to do?
- What's easy for you that's hard for others?
- What challenges have you overcome?

Make a list and **shoot for at least 20 to 30 ideas.** Then go through them and see what stands out.

Some will be obvious. Some might surprise you. And some might be things you're great at but **don't want to build a business around**. And that's just as valuable to know.

The goal here is to **find the overlap between what you're good at, what people need, and what you actually want to do.**

Because once you do, you're in a position to create something **people will pay for**—and more importantly, something you'll actually enjoy building.

TURNING YOUR BUSINESS IDEA INTO A PROFITABLE INCOME ENGINE

Profitability doesn't happen by accident. It's built through intentional strategy. Once you have a great product, you need a clear path to **convert visitors into buyers**. That includes:

- **Sales Pages** that clearly explain the value of your offer.
- **Email Sequences** that nurture leads and build trust.
- **Automated Funnels** that guide potential customers through the buying journey.

When done right, these elements allow you to step away while your business continues to generate revenue.

NEXT STEPS

Now that you understand the **4P Framework**, it's time to apply it. It starts with getting clear on *who you serve*. In the next chapter, we'll dive into finding your ideal audience and crafting a positioning statement that makes your business irresistible to the right people.

Let's keep going!

CHAPTER 3
WHO YOU SERVE AND WHY IT MATTERS

THE TWO DIMENSIONS OF THE "PERSON" YOU NEED TO CONSIDER: YOU AND YOUR AUDIENCE

Before you can create a profitable autopilot product, you need to know two things: who you are and who you serve. These two factors shape everything from your messaging to your product offerings.

- **You:** What are your skills, experiences, and passions? What unique perspective do you bring to the table?
- **Your Audience:** Who do you want to help? What problems do they face, and how can you provide a solution?

WHY AUDIENCE MATTERS

Your audience dictates everything:

- What problems you solve
- What language you use in your marketing
- Where you focus your promotional efforts
- How you price and package your products

If you try to sell to everyone, you'll sell to no one. Your goal is to create a message so specific that your ideal customer feels like you're speaking directly to them.

DEFINING YOUR IDEAL CUSTOMER

Ask yourself these questions:

Who do I enjoy helping the most?

What problems are they struggling with?

Where do they spend time online?

What type of content do they engage with?

What solutions are they already paying for?

THE POWER OF NICHE MARKETS

Many people fear niching down, thinking it limits opportunities. The opposite is true. Niching allows you to:

- Stand out in a crowded market
- Charge premium prices
- Build authority faster

For example, instead of being a "business coach," you could be a "business coach for freelance writers looking to land high-ticket clients." That specificity makes you the go-to expert for a particular group.

WHERE TO FIND YOUR AUDIENCE

Your ideal customers are already hanging out somewhere. You just need to find them. Some common places include:

- Facebook groups
- Subreddits
- LinkedIn communities
- YouTube channels
- Industry blogs

VALIDATING YOUR AUDIENCE

Before creating your product, validate demand by:

- Posting questions in relevant groups
- Engaging in conversations about their struggles
- Offering a free resource to gauge interest

If people respond positively, you know you're on the right track.

FINDING THE RIGHT NICHE

Choosing the right niche is about balancing passion with profitability. A successful niche has three key elements:

A real problem: Your audience must have a challenge they're eager to solve.

A willing-to-pay market: They must be willing to invest in a solution.

Alignment with your expertise: You should have experience or knowledge in this area.

And that brings me to this helpful tool I like to use to get clarity on *what exactly* I do, *who* I'm serving, and *how* I help them achieve their goals.

THE POSITIONING STATEMENT FORMULA

To clarify your niche and value proposition, use this simple formula:

I help [niche] achieve [desired result] through [your proven process], even if [common objection].

This helps you define your business in a way that's clear and compelling.

You can see how this works clearly when I fill in the blanks with my own business:

„I help musicians release radio-ready music through my step-by-step mixing process, even if they only have a home studio."

This positioning directly addresses a **common objection** in my industry—the outdated belief that **home studios can't produce professional-quality music.**

Not as much today as it used to be, but for a long time, home studios were seen as **low-quality, amateur demo spaces.** If you weren't recording in a commercial studio, your music wasn't taken seriously.

But that's simply **not true anymore.**

Today, with the right approach, **you can achieve high-quality, professional results from a home studio.** That's a **major limiting belief** I work to break for my audience. I know it's possible because I've helped countless musicians do it.

And I can prove it.

I have a Spotify playlist full of artists who have mixed and released their music using **only** a home studio setup. The results speak for themselves.

So when you're crafting your positioning, start by filling in the positioning statement:

„I help [your audience] achieve [specific result] through [your unique method], even if [common objection]."

Think about who **you** want to help, what **problem** you're solving, and what **limiting belief** you need to overcome for them. Once you have that dialed in, your messaging becomes much more powerful.

UNDERSTANDING YOUR CUSTOMERS: THE CUSTOMER CANVAS

All marketing revolves around one thing: **your customers.** If you don't understand them, their problems, and what they truly want, you'll struggle to create a business that resonates.

This is where the **Customer Canvas** comes in.

I developed this framework as a more **customer-centric** version of the **Lean Canvas**, which you may be familiar with from the startup world. It's also similar to the **Small Business Canvas**, but my focus was to make it completely **customer-driven.**

Let's go through it step by step.

1. THE PROBLEM—EVERY BUSINESS SOLVES A PROBLEM

All businesses exist to **solve a problem.**

For **Audio Issues**, I solve the problem of **muddy mixes** for home studio musicians. My business helps people **achieve professional-sounding music** and eliminates the frustration of mixes that don't sound right.

So when you're thinking about what product or business to create, ask yourself:

- What problem are you solving?
- Why does it matter to your customers?
- What pain are they experiencing that your product or service can eliminate?

2. HOPES, DREAMS, PAINS, AND FEARS— UNDERSTANDING EMOTIONS

Beyond the problem itself, you need to understand **how your customers feel.**

What are they **hoping** to achieve by solving this problem? What are they **afraid** will happen if they don't?

For my audience, one of their biggest fears is **sharing their music and realizing it sounds terrible.**

Imagine working on a song for months, playing it on a different set of speakers, and suddenly realizing it's full of mixing issues. Worse, imagine being at a party, your song comes on, and instead of feeling proud, you're just praying it ends as quickly as possible because you **hate how it sounds.**

That's a real **fear and pain** for many musicians. And that's why I focus on helping my audience feel **confident** that when they release their music, it will **sound great everywhere.**

So when you're thinking about your audience:

- What are their biggest hopes and dreams?
- What fears and pains are they trying to avoid?
- How does your product help them feel more confident and successful?

3. THE RESULT—WHAT TANGIBLE OUTCOME DO YOU PROVIDE?

You need to offer a **clear, tangible result** to your customers.

For **Audio Issues**, the result is simple:

"I help home studio musicians create radio-ready records"

My goal is to make sure that when you put your song on **Spotify, Apple Music, or anywhere else,** it sounds polished and professional. That's the end result I provide.

What's the clear, measurable outcome that your business or product delivers?

4. INTERESTS AND WORLDVIEW—WHO ARE YOUR PEOPLE?

"People like us do things like this" - Seth Godin

Every industry has its **schools of thought**–different perspectives that often clash on how things should be done.

In the audio industry, there are two clear camps.

On one side, you have the old-school commercial studio owners–the curmudgeons with their 48-channel mixing desks, convinced that no good music has been made since 1978. They spend their time online railing against modern production techniques, bemoaning the „decline of quality" in music, and insisting that **you can't make a good record in a home studio.**

To them, if you haven't invested at least $20,000 in pro gear, you're not serious about making music.

I want **nothing** to do with those people.

They are **not** my audience. They are difficult to teach, resistant to new ideas, and set in their ways. And honestly? That's fine. I'm not here to convince them.

Because there's another school of thought—the one I serve.

A few years ago, Billie Eilish and Finneas recorded an album in their home studio using budget gear, improper speaker placement, and an acoustically questionable set-up. And then?

They swept the Grammys for the "home studio" album. Suck it commercial studio curmudgeons.

There's a picture of them struggling to hold all of their awards in their arms, and it proves a simple but undeniable point: **you can make great music in a home studio.**

If your music is good, it doesn't matter whether your gear is expensive or not.

Those are my people. The musicians who believe in using what they have. The producers who care more about creativity than gatekeeping. The artists who know that great music isn't about how much you spend, but how well you use the tools available to you.

DEFINING YOUR AUDIENCE'S WORLDVIEW

This kind of division exists in **every** industry. There are different schools of thought, different camps, and different ways people believe you should achieve success.

Take **nutrition**, for example.

You've got **paleo, keto, low-carb, slow-carb, plant-based, intermittent fasting**—each with their own set of beliefs about what works and why. The people in these groups **self-identify** with their approach, and once they've picked a side, they rarely budge.

The same happens in business, fitness, self-improvement, and nearly every other field.

So when you're building your business, ask yourself:

- Who do I actually want to serve?
- What worldview do they have?
- What do they believe about success in this space?
- And just as importantly—who do I NOT want to serve?

Not everyone will align with your perspective, and **that's a good thing.**

By defining your audience's worldview, you're not just attracting the right people—you're filtering out the wrong ones. The people who will fight you on every idea, resist your methods, and never truly embrace what you're trying to teach.

And when you find your people? Your work becomes **easier, more enjoyable, and far more impactful.**

5. TRAFFIC SOURCES—WHERE DO YOUR CUSTOMERS HANG OUT?

Once you know **who** your audience is, you need to find **where** they spend their time.

Most of this happens online, which makes it easier to **get in front of them** if you know where to look.

Ask yourself:

- What Facebook groups are they in?
- What YouTube channels do they follow?
- What blogs do they read?
- What Instagram accounts do they engage with?

If you don't know the answers to these questions, spend some time researching. Because if you don't know where they are, you won't be able to reach them effectively.

6. COMPETITION AND COLLABORATION— WHY YOUR COMPETITORS CAN BE YOUR PARTNERS

A lot of people get **intimidated** by competition. But the truth is, competition is **a good thing.**

It means there's **a market.**

And don't dismiss the idea that **your competition can also be your collaborator.**

A great example: A few years ago, I partnered with **Graham Cochrane** from **The Recording Revolution**. He created a course with Grammy-winning producer **Jacquire King**, called *Record Making with Jacquire King*.

Now, you might think, „Wait...The Recording Revolution is a direct competitor to Audio Issues!"

But instead of seeing them as competition, I looked for a way to **collaborate.**

Instead of getting frustrated that they made a great course before I did, I became an **affiliate** for them.

I promoted their course to my audience, knowing it was a valuable resource. They had already spent **hundreds of hours** and **thousands of dollars** creating this high-quality product. Instead of competing, I partnered with them, sent out a few emails, and earned commissions from every sale.

No production costs. No stress. Just a win-win collaboration that made an extra $7,000 that month.

So when you're thinking about competition:

- Who are the key players in your industry?

- Are there ways to partner with them instead of competing?
- Do they have products you can promote before you create your own?
- Can you offer something complementary to what they already sell?

FINAL THOUGHTS

If you take the time to go through these steps, you'll have a **clear picture of your ideal customer and how to serve them.**

What problem are you solving?

What emotions (hopes, dreams, fears) drive your customers?

What tangible result do you offer?

Who are your people—and who aren't?

Where do they spend their time online?

How can you turn competitors into collaborators?

When you answer these questions, your marketing becomes **10x easier.** You'll know **exactly** what to say, who to talk to, and where to find them.

And when you do that, **selling becomes effortless.**

In the next chapter, we'll break down the process of creating a product that **sells itself**, so you can generate passive income without constantly chasing new clients.

NEXT STEPS

Now that you understand your audience and positioning, we'll move on to building your platform and attracting the right people to your business.

CHAPTER 4
PLATFORMS, AUDIENCES, AND VISIBILITY

When it comes to marketing, there are countless strategies, tactics, and systems you could follow. But trying to do **everything at once** is a recipe for burnout.

That's why I focus on **one** main approach: **The inbound marketing system.**

INBOUND MARKETING: BRINGING YOUR AUDIENCE TO YOU

Inbound marketing combines multiple marketing techniques in a way that's simple to understand and execute, without overwhelming you. The core idea? You create a platform, find your audience where they already are, and bring them back to your platform.

It's all about getting them to **come inbound** to you.

YOUR PLATFORM: THE HUB OF YOUR MARKETING SYSTEM

Think of your marketing system like a wheel.

At the **center** is your **platform**. Your **sphere of influence**. This usually consists of:

- Your email list (your most valuable asset)
- Your website
- A landing page that directs people to your offers

Everything you do feeds back to this hub, where you can build deeper relationships with your audience and promote your products or services.

YOUR MARKETING CHANNELS: THE SPOKES OF THE WHEEL

The **marketing channels**—where you actually **reach your audience**—are the **spokes** of the wheel.

This could be:

- TikTok
- Instagram
- Facebook
- YouTube
- Twitter/X
- Podcasts
- Newer platforms like BlueSky or Threads

Any of these can work. **But everything does not.**

START SMALL, THEN EXPAND

If you try to be **everywhere at once**, you'll spread yourself too thin. It will be hard to gain traction, and you'll likely burn out fast.

Instead, **start with just one or two platforms** where your audience is **already active.** Get comfortable. Build momentum. Once you establish a presence, you can **expand strategically.**

Marketing isn't about doing **everything**—it's about doing **the right things, consistently.**

CHOOSING THE RIGHT CONTENT PLATFORM FOR YOU

When creating content, **choose a platform that aligns with your strengths and interests.**

- **If you love to talk**, then podcasts might be the perfect fit for you.
- **If you enjoy making short, engaging videos**, TikTok and Instagram are great platforms to explore.
- **If you prefer in-depth, long-form content**, a YouTube channel could be the way to go.
- **If writing is your strength**, platforms like **Medium or Substack** are great options for publishing detailed articles and newsletters.

The key is to **pick a format that feels natural to you**, because if you try to do **all of these things at once, you'll burn out.** I guarantee it.

For instance, I am primarily a writer, and I started building an audience as a blogger. I never felt comfortable on camera until recently, and starting a podcast just didn't click with me as well as writing down my thoughts. Has that stopped me from carving out a small sliver of success in my field? **Not at all.**

And today, after thousands of hours of writing and probably a million words, I'm exploring YouTube as a medium because I feel like that's the best place to spread my message and reach a new, different audience.

HOW THIS ALL COMES TOGETHER

Your content should act as a **bridge** between your audience and your business.

- You pick a **traffic channel** (your content platform of choice).
- You put your **message out there** through valuable content.
- Some of the people who see your content will **take the next step**—they'll visit your website, check out your services, or explore your product offerings.
- A portion of those people will **become customers and clients.**

That's really **all** marketing is.

Not everyone who sees your content will convert, but that's okay. If 1,000 people see your message, not all of them will become customers right away. But a handful will be the right fit, and those are the people you're looking for.

The goal is **not** to attract everyone. The goal is to **attract the right people**—the ones who resonate with your message and are genuinely interested in what you have to offer.

CASE STUDY: HOW A TOILET SCROLL TURNED ME INTO A SUPERFAN (AND WHAT THAT MEANS FOR YOUR MARKETING)

Let me tell you a story to illustrate the marketing funnel in detail.

It starts in the most sacred place of modern solitude: the bathroom.

Yup. The one place my tyrant toddler can't find me. It's also where I, like 90% of the planet, doom scroll in peace. On one such scroll session, I came across a short video by a musician named Connor Price. I'd never heard of him. His

music wasn't something Spotify thought I'd like. And yet…
I became a fan.

Not just a casual fan, either. A full-fledged, "tell my friends
and spend money on his stuff" fan.

This wasn't some grand marketing campaign or massive
ad budget at play. It was just a smart artist using the right
content in the right place at the right time.

Let's break it down and reverse-engineer how this unknown
artist caught my attention—and how you can do the same
for your music.

1. THE ALGORITHM'S CHICKEN NUGGET PROBLEM

Spotify's recommendation engine is like a new parent trying to get their toddler to eat broccoli.

It'll give you *tiny* doses of new music, but mostly it serves
up the same musical Chicken McNuggets. Your tried-
and-true playlists, favorite bands, and comforting old-
school jams.

Breaking into that comfort zone is like trying to get someone to switch pizza toppings after 20 years of pepperoni
loyalty. And yet, somehow, Connor Price got through to me,
but not on Spotify.

2. THE AWARENESS STAGE: THE FIRST VIDEO HIT

It all started with a funny, short-form video. Connor played both the role of an artist entering a studio and the producer behind the desk. Classic content setup, but well done. A quick sketch, a beat, and a clever ending with his song playing. I chuckled. Then I moved on with my life outside the bathroom.

But Meta's robots took note. I'd watched the full reel. Now, my feed had been flagged. And the next time I escaped parenting to my porcelain think tank, boom. Connor showed up again.

3. THE ENGAGEMENT STAGE: FAMILIARITY BREEDS…INTEREST?

The algorithm got me. It knew I'd watch another one of these sketches. And every reel the algorithm fed me made me more interested in the songs that he used in his reels.

By the third or fourth video, I did what every marketer dreams of: I clicked through to his profile. I followed him. And the algorithm gods rejoiced. Somewhere, a Meta intern probably got a raise.

In funnel-speak, I'd moved from "awareness" to "engagement." I wasn't just vaguely amused anymore—I was watching. Actively. Repeatedly. Willingly.

4. THE ACTION STAGE: STREAMING ON SPOTIFY

Now that I was a follower, his content appeared even more frequently. I got to know him, his personality, and his music. Eventually, I became so invested that I searched for him on Spotify and followed him there as well.

Cue the Spotify robots high-fiving the Facebook robots.

This was the moment every musician hopes for: I'd taken action. I'd crossed over from passive scroller to engaged listener.

5. The Superfan Stage: When the Song Hits Hard

Here's where things went from "this is catchy" to "I need to tell other people about this."

Connor released a song inspired by his newborn son, Jude. As a dad to a two-year-old daughter at the time, I wasn't ready. That song *wrecked me*.

It was honest, emotional, and beautifully done. It mirrored my own experience. That's when it clicked: I wasn't just a fan of the music. I was a fan of *him*.

So I went to his website, and wouldn't you know—it had something perfect for me to buy. A "dad hat" baseball cap. And I did. Because when someone makes you *feel* something, paying them feels like saying thank you.

SO WHAT CAN YOU LEARN FROM THIS?

Connor Price didn't spam me. He didn't beg me to check out his "fire new single." He just showed up where I was, told short, funny stories that featured his music, and stayed consistent.

Here's how you can do the same:

Create Shareable Content. This isn't just applicable to musical artists. You can create mini-stories, sketches, and behind-the-scenes reels that *feature* your message. Think of the content as the trailer; your product is the movie.

Make Content That's Creative. Connor's skits were engaging, funny, and smart. If the content itself is entertaining, people will stick around long enough.

Be Consistent. I saw multiple videos before I followed him. One video isn't a strategy—it's a fluke. Build a *catalog* of content so the algorithm has ammo.

Be Easy to Find. Don't make people hunt you down. Connor was just a search away on Spotify and easy to follow on social media. Clean up your profiles. Use the same name everywhere. Make it stupid simple to find you.

Give People a Way to Support You. Streaming pennies won't pay your rent. Monetizing a YouTube channel is not a proper revenue stream unless you have millions of views. Have merch. Have a product. Offer *something* people can buy when they want to say, "Thank you for making me feel something."

THINK OF YOUR BUSINESS LIKE AN ARTIST

The content you make *about* your business is also art. It's a performance, a story, a way in. Think of your short videos as the door, and your business as the beautiful, weird, emotional house they get to explore once they step inside.

And just like I did with Connor Price, someone out there might be one song (and one bathroom scroll) away from becoming your next true fan.

WHERE YOUR AUDIENCE IS AND HOW TO FIND THEM

Not all platforms are created equal. Your audience is already **hanging out** somewhere online—you just need to figure out where.

STRATEGIES TO IDENTIFY YOUR AUDIENCE'S PREFERRED PLATFORM:

Observe Competitors - Look at where similar businesses are growing their audience.

Engage in Online Communities - Participate in relevant Facebook groups, Reddit threads, and LinkedIn discussions.

Analyze Search Behavior - Use tools like Google Trends and keyword research to find out what people are searching for.

Survey Your Existing Audience - If you have a small email list or social following, ask them where they consume content.

For example, a **graphic designer** looking to sell digital templates might find that their audience prefers **Pinterest and Instagram**, where visual content thrives.

Meanwhile, a **business consultant** may have better traction on **LinkedIn** and through an email newsletter.

For myself, I've always found my audience on Facebook and Instagram and that's where most of my leads come from. However, there's a thriving community of home studio musicians and bedroom producers on Reddit, and I tend to lurk there too, gathering ideas for content and questions to answer.

On the flipside, I've written a bunch of business and marketing articles on Medium, and that's always felt like a good place to share that type of content. But you won't find a lot of music producers there, so it's not a platform I would pick to grow my audience for the audio business.

THE LEAD MAGNET FUNNEL FRAMEWORK: HOW TO GENERATE LEADS AND CUSTOMERS

One of the most effective ways to build an audience and generate sales is through what I call the **Lead Magnet Funnel Framework.**

And here's the thing—you're already proof that it works.

HOW YOU GOT HERE

Think about it. What brought you here today?

Here's what happened:

- I either **ran an ad** or **sent an email** that led you to a **landing page.**
- That page encouraged you to buy this book.
- You received a **thank you email.**
- Then, you got a **reminder email** with either a reminder to read the book, a link to a complementary product, or both.
- And now, **here you are.**

That's **the Lead Magnet Funnel Framework in action.**

But it's not just for **books**—you can use this same system to sell **masterclasses, courses, services, or anything else.** It's how I've launched everything online, whether it be a workshop, a free checklist, or a paid online course.

It's a **repeatable strategy** for generating leads and turning them into customers.

TWO SCHOOLS OF THOUGHT ON BUILDING YOUR EMAIL LIST

When it comes to attracting leads—**interested people who might buy from you**—there are two main approaches.

1. THE FREE LEAD MAGNET STRATEGY

This is the most common method. You offer **something valuable for free** in exchange for an email address.

You've seen this before. In fact, you've probably signed up for free resources yourself.

For example, at **Audio Issues**, I offer a **Quick Mixing Checklist**—a **free PDF** with **110 mixing tips** that people can download instantly.

Here's how it works:

- You sign up for the checklist.
- You join my **email list.**
- You receive **valuable content** (some of my best blog posts, tips, and insights).
- You also receive **offers** for my products, like *Step By Step Mixing* or *Easy Mix Approach.*

Some people on the list will eventually buy.

Why does this work?

- It's **easier** to build a list when you offer something for free.
- People are more likely to say **yes** to a free resource.

What's the downside?

- Not everyone on the list will become a customer.
- Some will just want the freebie and never buy.

But here's something to keep in mind: **Even freebie seekers can bring you value.**

They might **never buy from you**, but if they love your content, they might **recommend it to someone else** who **will** make a purchase. Word-of-mouth marketing is powerful, and you never know where your next customer might come from.

2. THE LOW-TICKET PRODUCT STRATEGY

The other school of thought is to **sell something right away** instead of offering a freebie.

Instead of giving away a lead magnet, you offer a **low-ticket product**—something small but valuable.

The trade-off:

- It's **harder** to grow a large list with this method because people are less likely to pay upfront.
- You'll have to spend **more on ads** to get paying customers.

For example:

- With a free lead magnet, you might spend **$1 per subscriber.**
- With a paid offer, you might need to spend **$10-$15** (or more, depending on your industry) per customer.

That means if you're running ads, you need to price your product high enough to cover your costs and make a profit.

But the **upside** is that this method can be **more profitable upfront.**

WHY PAID CUSTOMERS ARE MORE VALUABLE

There's a key psychological factor at play here—**customers behave differently from freebie seekers.**

Customers are more engaged.

- They're more likely to **open your emails.**
- They already see value in what you offer because they've **spent money with you.**
- They're **more likely to buy again.**

Think about it—someone who has **already bought from you** is much more likely to **purchase another product** than someone who has never spent a dollar with you.

This is why **repeat customers** are the foundation of a sustainable business.

But here's the catch: **This only works if your first product is actually good.**

If your first product **sucks**, don't expect repeat buyers. Simple as that.

THE LEAD MAGNET FUNNEL IN ACTION: A REAL-WORLD EXAMPLE

So how does this work in practice? **Simple.**

It starts with an **ad**, which leads to a **landing page**, which leads to a **confirmation page**, followed by **emails**, and finally, a **sales page**. That's the **Lead Magnet Funnel Framework** in action.

Let me walk you through a **real example** from my business.

STEP 1: THE AD THAT ATTRACTS THE RIGHT AUDIENCE

One of the most effective lead magnets I offer is a **free EQ Cheat Sheet**.

I help a lot of people with **equalization (EQ)**. It's one of the most common struggles for musicians and producers. I even have a full **EQ software plug-in** that helps people understand the **frequency spectrum** better.

But it **all starts with a simple ad.**

The ad offers a **free cheat sheet** that helps musicians quickly grasp the basics of EQ. It's a **valuable, quick-win resource** that solves an immediate problem.

STEP 2: THE LANDING PAGE THAT CONVERTS

When someone clicks on the ad, they land on a **dedicated landing page**.

This page is designed with a clear, benefit-driven headline that immediately tells them what they'll get and why it matters.

Here's what's on the page:

- **A 3D image of the PDF** to make it visually appealing.
- **Bullet points** highlighting exactly what's inside.
- **Testimonials** for social proof—so they see that others have already benefited from it.
- A **value proposition**—I list the worth of the cheat sheet as **$19, but they get it for free.**

Why do I put a price on it, even though it's free?

Because **if you don't define your worth, others will do it for you**—and usually, they'll undervalue you. By showing that the resource has a real value, I reinforce its importance.

Once they sign up, they **immediately receive the PDF,** and now they're on my **email list.**

STEP 3: THE EMAIL SEQUENCE THAT BUILDS TRUST

Once someone has joined my email list, I already **know** they're interested in EQ. So what do I do? **I send them more valuable content about EQ.**

This makes perfect sense—if you signed up to learn about **Topic X**, you're likely **still interested** in Topic X.

So I continue providing:

- More useful EQ tips.
- Solutions to common EQ problems.
- Personal stories and insights.

Over time, these emails **build trust** and reinforce that I **know what I'm talking about.** And if someone actually applies my advice and sees their mixes improve, they're even more likely to **continue engaging** with my content.

WRITING AN EMAIL SEQUENCE THAT CONVERTS

A well-structured email sequence follows a **relationship-first approach**—delivering value, sharing your story, and naturally leading into your product offer.

Here's a **proven five-email sequence** to turn subscribers into buyers:

Welcome Email (Day 1):

- Thank them for downloading the lead magnet.
- Introduce yourself and your expertise.
- Set expectations for what's coming next.

Problem & Solution Email (Day 2-3):

- Address a core challenge your audience faces.
- Explain how your product solves this problem.
- Include a **soft CTA** (Call-to-Action) to check out your product.

Authority & Social Proof (Day 4-5):

- Share a success story or testimonial from someone who has used your product.
- Reinforce the transformation your product provides.
- Include a **stronger CTA** to encourage them to take action.

Address Objections (Day 6-7):

- Handle common concerns like price, time commitment, or effectiveness.
- Use FAQs or a case study to show real-world success.
- Provide a **limited-time incentive** (bonus, discount, extra support).

Final Call-to-Action (Day 8-9):

- Remind them why they signed up and what's at stake if they don't take action.
- Include a **final push** with urgency (e.g., "Doors close tomorrow!").
- Make it **easy to buy** with a clear CTA and simple check-out process.

STEP 4: THE SALES PITCH (WITHOUT BEING SPAMMY)

At the end of the email sequence (or sometimes throughout), I'll transition into an offer.

The logic is simple:

If you like my free content, you'll love my paid product.

My EQ plug-in goes beyond the cheat sheet. It's a practical tool that offers **more insights and more structured guidance** to help them improve their mixes.

Some emails are **purely value-based**, offering **free advice, tips, or personal stories**. Others are **more sales-driven**, introducing my product as a **logical next step**.

WHY SELLING IS HELPING

Many entrepreneurs struggle with selling because they associate it with pushy tactics and manipulation. But selling isn't about tricking people. It's about **helping them solve a problem**. If your product truly provides value, then offering it is a service, not an imposition.

Reframe selling by asking yourself:

- Does my product genuinely improve lives?
- Would I feel comfortable recommending this to a friend?
- Am I providing an honest solution rather than just making a sale?

When you see sales as a way to **serve** rather than just to profit, selling becomes much easier and more natural.

USING STORYTELLING TO BUILD TRUST

People don't buy products. They buy **stories and transformations**. The most effective way to sell is through compelling storytelling.

THE THREE-PART SALES STORY:

The Struggle: Start by identifying the problem your audience faces.

The Breakthrough: Share how you (or someone else) discovered the solution.

The Transformation: Show the tangible results they can expect after using your product.

Example:

- **Struggle:** "I used to spend hours trying to mix my music, only to end up frustrated with muddy, unprofessional tracks."
- **Breakthrough:** "After testing countless techniques, I found a simple framework that made mixing effortless."
- **Transformation:** "Now, my songs sound clear, polished, and radio-ready—without spending hours tweaking every setting."

When people see themselves in your story, they'll feel more **emotionally connected** to your product and trust that it can help them.

ETHICAL PERSUASION: ENCOURAGING ACTION WITHOUT MANIPULATION

Selling with integrity means **guiding** customers to the right decision without resorting to pressure or guilt. Here are some ethical persuasion techniques:

- **Scarcity (without false urgency):** "We only open enrollment twice a year."
- **Social Proof:** "Over 10,000 students have used this framework successfully."
- **Risk Reversal:** "30-day money-back guarantee—if it doesn't work for you, we'll refund every penny."

I've used variations of these risk reversals in all of my products:

- **Scarcity:** "This limited-time discount is only available twice a year."
- **Social Proof:** "Over 40,000 musicians like yourself have bought Step By Step Mixing to help them release their records."
- **Risk Reversal:** "Step By Step Mixing comes with a 100% risk-free money-back guarantee. You can even try all the tricks and keep the training for a full year before deciding whether you like them or not."

The goal is to create **confidence**, not pressure.

WHY I SHARE MY STORY

I tend to tell my story because **storytelling is one of the most powerful tools in business.**

You saw this at the beginning of this book. I shared some highlights of my professional journey through a story. Not just as a way to introduce myself, but to **build a connection** with you. Because at the end of the day, people don't just buy products. They buy from people they **trust**.

Storytelling makes you **real.** It makes you **relatable.** It reminds your audience that you're not just some AI robot sent to persuade them into buying something—they're engaging with a **real human** who has walked the same path, faced the same struggles, and found solutions that actually work.

And then, once that **trust is built**, I transition into selling.

Not with aggressive sales tactics. Not with spammy pitches. But with **a natural progression**—from story to solution.

That's why I always include **a few emails in my sequences that are more sales-driven** than pure value. Not because I want to push products for the sake of selling, but because I **genuinely believe in what I offer**. I know my products help people, and I know they can **make a real difference** in my audience's lives.

Storytelling isn't just a way to get attention—it's a way to **show people why your product matters.** And when you do that right, selling becomes effortless.

I **never** believe in spammy sales tactics. If you genuinely **believe in your product** and know it **will help your audience,** you should **sell with confidence.**

STEP 5: THE SALES PAGE THAT CONVERTS

The **final step** in the funnel is the **sales page**.

This page follows a similar structure to the lead magnet page but focuses on why the paid product is the ultimate solution.

- It has **a headline, subheading, and a hook** that clearly states the benefit.
- It includes **a video** that explains the product. I often add a short personal story as well.
- It features **images of the product.**
- It has **testimonials** from satisfied customers.

At this stage, many people **buy directly** from the email sequence.

TWO WAYS I SELL: LEAD MAGNETS VS. LOW-TICKET OFFERS

Like I mentioned before, there are **two schools of thought** when it comes to marketing funnels:

The Lead Magnet Approach—offering something for free, then nurturing people through email.

The Low-Ticket Product Approach—selling a **low-cost** product directly through ads.

I **do both.**

Some people sign up for the **free lead magnet** first and later buy the product. Others see **an ad for the paid product** and buy it immediately, even before they join my email list.

WHY THIS WORKS SO WELL

This system works because it's **diversified.**

Some customers need **more time** before they're ready to buy, so the **email sequence nurtures them.** Others are **ready to buy now**, so I sell directly through **low-ticket product ads.**

By running **both strategies**, I maximize my reach and **convert at different stages of the customer journey.**

WHICH STRATEGY SHOULD YOU USE?

- If you're focused on long-term audience growth, start with a free lead magnet.
- If you want to test an offer quickly and generate revenue **more quickly**, consider a low-ticket product.

Both methods work. It just depends on **your business goals, budget, and timeline.**

The key takeaway? **Have a system in place.** To build a sustainable business, you need **a strategy to attract leads, engage them, and convert them into paying customers.**

And the Lead Magnet Funnel Framework does exactly that.

KEY TAKEAWAYS: HOW YOU CAN APPLY THIS

If you're building a business, you need a **structured system** to attract leads and turn them into customers.

You can follow the **same framework** I use:

Create a valuable lead magnet (a free checklist, guide, template, etc.).

Drive traffic to a landing page through ads, social media, or content marketing.

Capture email addresses and deliver the lead magnet immediately.

Nurture your audience with helpful, engaging emails.

Introduce your paid offer as a natural next step.

Use a well-designed sales page to convert buyers.

If you want to test faster, you can also **sell a low-ticket product upfront** instead of a freebie.

NEXT STEPS

Now that you've chosen a platform and identified your target audience, it's time to **convert that visibility into revenue**.

CHAPTER 5
TURNING PROCRASTINATION INTO PROFIT

HOW I CREATED A $25,000 PRODUCT BY ACCIDENT

This is one of my favorite examples because it perfectly illustrates how I used **my own art and creativity as a musician** to create a product, almost by accident.

It all started with a song.

Back in December 2023, I recorded a song called „Sympathy." It's a song about loss, grief, and mourning—something I wrote 15 years ago but never got around to properly recording. Finally, I put a band together, got in the studio, and recorded the song.

I was super proud of it.

But then my entrepreneur brain kicked in.

THE CHALLENGE: HOW DO YOU MONETIZE A SONG?

People don't really **buy music** anymore. Sure, I'd love for people to listen to it. I like to tell people that I released "Sympathy" for everyone who's walking around with a hole in their heart where a loved one used to live.

So I hoped it would **connect with others who had lost some-one,** and that it would **mean something** to them.

And it did.

When I released the song, people reached out, saying how much the song resonated with them. And I loved that. But **streams and compliments don't pay the bills.**

So I asked myself, **how can I turn this into something that both:**

Earns back the money I spent on studio time and session musicians.

Creates something valuable for my audience while still showcasing the song.

THE UNEXPECTED ROADBLOCK: MY MIXING TEMPLATE

Before I finished producing the song, I was facing a different challenge.

I had just bought a new computer and reinstalled all my audio software. But my mixing template—the one I use to streamline my workflow—was on my old computer.

I thought, *No big deal. I'll just create a new template.*

So I put „**Create New Mixing Template**" on my **to-do list.**

And then... I did nothing.

That task just sat there. Every week, I moved it to „**next Friday.**" And then the **Friday after that.**

I had a song I wanted to mix and release, but I was letting a seemingly **insignificant task**–creating a new mixing template–get in the way.

THE BREAKTHROUGH: TURNING A CHORE INTO A PRODUCT

Finally, I had a realization:

I have an audience of 40,000-50,000 home studio musicians and bedroom producers, all of whom are passionate about mixing.

If I had this problem–struggling to create an efficient workflow–**they probably did too.**

So I asked myself:

- What if I turned this into a live class?
- What if I showed my audience how I build my own mixing template?

- What if, by the end of the class, not only would I have my template, but they would also know how to create their own?

And that's exactly what I did.

THE EASY MIX APPROACH: A PRODUCT BORN FROM PROCRASTINATION

I launched and sold tickets to a **live class**, where I taught:

- How to create a mixing template from scratch.
- How to use presets to get fast, consistent results.
- How to streamline your workflow as an audio engineer.

At the end of it, I had my **new mixing template**—the one I had been procrastinating on for weeks.

And my audience? **They got a masterclass on productivity, efficiency, and better mixing.**

That live session turned into **The Easy Mix Approach**: a **two-hour training** that also includes downloadable mixing templates, which my students can **easily integrate** into their own software.

THE SURPRISING SUCCESS: $25,000+ IN SALES

Since launching the product, **The Easy Mix Approach has generated over $25,000 in sales to date.**

All because I was **procrastinating.**

It's kind of ironic—I was struggling with productivity, so I ended up creating a **productivity tool** that helped **both me and my audience.**

And it didn't take a huge marketing push.

I sent out **a few emails** to my list, hosted a **live training,** packaged it into **a digital product**, put it on a **sales page,** and... that was it.

It still sells copies **all the time,** becoming one of my best-selling products and a brand-new income stream for my business.

THE LESSON: MONETIZE WHAT YOU'RE ALREADY DOING

The biggest takeaway?

If you're struggling to come up with product ideas, **look at what you're already doing.**

- What tasks are you **already working on** that others might find valuable?
- What **problems are you solving** for yourself that others need help with?
- Can you **involve your audience** in the process and make it a product?

You don't have to **reinvent the wheel**—sometimes, the best products come from **solving your own challenges** in real-time.

HOW TO PRODUCTIZE YOUR CREATIVITY INTO A PRODUCT THAT SELLS ITSELF

Let's discuss how you can do something similar and turn your creativity into a product you can sell.

There are **a lot** of different products you can create. And I've created **most of them** in some way or another. The Easy Mix Approach is just one example.

I've written **books**.

I've created **templates and mini-courses**.

I've run **membership sites**.

I've done **one-off workshops** and **longer, more in-depth courses**.

I've even created **software** products.

There are also **low-content books**, which are an interesting category of products. These are things like **journals, action workbooks, and guided planners**—books that provide structure and guidance rather than traditional long-form content.

Funny story: One of the first products I ever made was a low-content book, and I think I sold less than 10 copies in its lifetime. Of course, just because I failed at creating this type of product doesn't mean there aren't hugely successful journals, planners and workbooks out there. It didn't work for me, but it might just be the perfect product for your market.

And remember, although my product launch back then was a failure, I still learned a great deal about product creation, customer discovery, and marketing. Knowledge I used after I picked myself up and tried again.

REAL-WORLD EXAMPLES FROM MY BUSINESS

Here are a few examples of successful products I created in my own business:

- **Books:** *Step By Step Mixing*—a guide that helps musicians improve their mixes. At the time of writing, it has 1,244 ratings, averaging a 4.5-star rating. Not too shabby for a no-name engineer from Iceland.

- **Flagship courses:** *Mix Finisher Formula*–a complete start-to-finish video program on mixing in the home studio. At last count it had about 490 students who had paid around $297 each.
- **Membership Community:** *The Insiders Community*–a $29/month membership I ran for several years, offering coaching calls and direct support (some of you reading this may have even been part of it!). This generated around $18,000 per year in recurring revenue before I closed it down to focus on other things.
- **Software:** *Audio Issues EQ*–a tool that helps users understand the frequency spectrum. This has been one of my most successful products because it goes beyond just selling knowledge. It's a tool they can use to help them achieve their goals of making good music. Knowledge alone doesn't sell as well as it used to because you can learn most things for free on YouTube, but bundling your expertise with a tool is something you can't get on YouTube or through knowledge alone.

Each of these products **solves a specific problem** for my audience, but they all connect to **one core problem**:

Helping musicians avoid muddy mixes and confidently make better music they're proud to release.

THE KEY TO CREATING PRODUCTS THAT SELL

The biggest takeaway here? **All of my products solve the same overarching problem, but in different ways.**

And that's the approach you should take when creating products for your own business. Identify the core problem your audience struggles with, and develop multiple solutions in various formats.

Some people **prefer reading** a book. Others **want video training**. Some **like interactive coaching**, while others **want software tools** that simplify the process.

You don't have to create everything at once, but the more ways you can package your expertise, the more opportunities you have to serve your audience—and the more revenue streams you can create.

THE „SIMPLE SOLUTION" APPROACH TO DIGITAL PRODUCTS

The best-selling products don't have to be complex. In fact, some of the most profitable digital products solve a single, well-defined problem in the simplest way possible.

The key is **clarity**: Knowing exactly what problem your product solves and making that clear to your audience.

CHOOSING THE RIGHT TYPE OF PRODUCT

When it comes to autopilot products, there are multiple options, but the right one depends on your strengths and audience preferences. Here are some of the most effective types:

- **E-books & Guides** – Great for quick consumption and easy entry-level pricing.
- **Online Courses** – Higher perceived value and ideal for in-depth learning.
- **Templates & Toolkits** – Done-for-you resources that save people time and effort.
- **Memberships & Subscriptions** – A recurring revenue model that offers ongoing value.
- **Software & Digital Tools** – High perceived value and scalable growth potential.

The key is to pick the **simplest** product that provides a clear solution to your audience's problem.

So before you move on to the next chapter, brainstorm what type of product you want to focus on creating first.

CHAPTER 6

THE THREE-WEEK AUTO-PILOT PRODUCT ROADMAP

TURNING YOUR IDEAS INTO PROFITABLE PRODUCTS

Creating a product doesn't have to take months or years. You can **validate, build, and launch** a product in just **three weeks** by following a structured approach.

This roadmap will help you go from an idea to a **real, sellable product** while testing demand along the way.

This process is exactly how I've created many of my own products, like the aforementioned Easy Mix Approach. As you know, not every product was a home run, but by following this system, I learned how to **test, iterate, and improve** over time.

WEEK 1: UNDERSTAND YOUR CUSTOMER & DEVELOP YOUR PRODUCT IDEA

The first step is **defining the problem you want to solve.**

Every successful product exists because it solves a specific problem for a specific audience. Ask yourself:

- What problem do my customers struggle with?
- What's a simple way I can help them solve part of that problem?
- What's a product I can create quickly and easily?

For example, I love writing books—I've written a lot of them—but they take **a long time** to complete. So if I'm looking for **quick results**, writing a book isn't the best approach. Instead, I'll create:

- A class
- A template
- A mini-course

These are **faster to produce** and still provide **real value.**

START SMALL—SOLVE A PIECE OF THE PROBLEM

You don't have to create **a massive, comprehensive product** right away. Instead, solve **a small piece of a larger problem.**

For example, when I created the **Easy Mix Approach**, I didn't try to teach everything about mixing. I focused on **one key aspect—building a mixing template.** That solved a specific problem for my audience in a **quick, actionable** way.

TEST DEMAND WITH A FREE OFFER

Before investing too much time, you need to determine if people actually **care** about your idea. The easiest way?

- Create a landing page for a free product or a webinar related to your idea.
- Share it in relevant Facebook groups, blog posts, or email lists.
- Run low-budget ads to drive traffic to it.

If **nobody signs up**, that's a red flag—you might need to adjust your idea. But if people **do** sign up, you now have an audience that's interested in what you're creating.

WEEK 2: BUILD MOMENTUM & CREATE YOUR SALES PAGE

Now that you know people are interested, it's time to **build on that momentum.**

- **Continue posting content** about the problem your product solves.
- **Keep running ads or sharing links** to your landing page.
- **Start sending emails** to your new subscribers.

USE STORYTELLING TO REINFORCE YOUR EXPERTISE

People don't just buy information—they buy information that's put together in an easy-to-understand way that they can apply to get results.

Not only that, but they buy **from people they trust.**

This is where **storytelling comes in.**

In my emails, I always share my **personal experiences**. I tell people how I've **struggled with the same problems** they're facing, how I found a solution, and how I'm now helping others do the same.

For example, before launching the **Easy Mix Approach**, I realized that my audience was highly interested in **mixing templates**. I had a **blog post** that explained how to create a mixing template, and whenever I mentioned it in my emails, the open rates and click-through rates would skyrocket.

That told me: **People are interested in this topic, so they might be willing to buy a deeper, more detailed version of it.**

CREATE A PAID VERSION OF YOUR FREE PRODUCT

Once you've built an engaged audience, the next step is to **upgrade your free product into a premium version.**

Take what's already working and **enhance it:**

- Add more depth
- Provide step-by-step instructions
- Include video walkthroughs or downloadable tools

Then, create a **sales page** for this upgraded version.

For example, I started with a **free blog post** about mixing templates. Once I saw people were highly engaged, I expanded it into **Easy Mix Approach**–a full **two-hour masterclass** with downloadable templates. As I mentioned earlier, that product has since generated **over $25,000.**

SET UP YOUR PAYMENT SYSTEM

Once your sales page is ready, make sure you have a way to **collect payments.**

You'll need:

- **Stripe, Square or PayPal** (most common)
- **A shopping cart software.**

At the time of writing, I use Kajabi, but there are many great options available that you can use. What you need is the ability to sell your product through a sales page, take payment from a checkout page, and deliver your product through an automated system.

At this point, your product is **ready to launch.**

WEEK 3: LAUNCH, TEST, AND IMPROVE

Now it's time to **get your product in front of people**.

- Send a launch email to your list.
- Share your thoughts on your social media channels.
- Run ads to your sales page.

Some products will **take off immediately**. Others will need **adjustments**. That's completely normal.

TEST, REFLECT, AND REPEAT

Not every product is going to be a home run. Trust me, I've created **tons** of online products over the last 15 years, and not all of them worked.

Sometimes I:

- **Made incorrect assumptions** about what people wanted.
- **Priced a product too low** (so people didn't see its value).
- **Priced it too high** (so people hesitated to buy).

This is all part of the process.

When something **doesn't work**, go back to your audience and ask:

- What else do you need help with?
- What would make this product more valuable?
- What's your next big challenge?

SOLVING ONE PROBLEM LEADS TO ANOTHER: CREATING PRODUCTS THAT GROW WITH YOUR AUDIENCE

You don't have to sell to new customers all the time. Sometimes it's easier to sell more products to an audience that already knows, likes, and trusts you. The trick is to find new problems to solve and package your products accordingly, based on where they are in their journey.

Let's imagine you have a business in the music industry like me, and your audience are all home studio musicians and bedroom producers.

Jake is a passionate musician with a dream. He wants to **write and record his first song.**

At first, Jake has **one** big problem: **He doesn't know how to write a song.**

So, as a smart business owner, you create a simple solution—maybe a songwriting workbook or a step-by-step course that helps them go from scattered lyric ideas to a fully structured song.

He buys it, follows your framework, and after a few weeks of inspiration (and a little procrastination), he finally **finishes his song.**

Victory!

However, Jake now faces **a new problem.**

„OKAY... NOW WHAT?"

Jake quickly realizes writing the song was just **the first step.** Now, he has to **record and mix** it.

He opens his DAW (Digital Audio Workstation), stares at the screen, and **panics.** *Why do these tracks look like a science experiment?* He plays around with some EQ settings, throws a random reverb on his vocals, and after hours of tweaking, his mix **still sounds like it was recorded inside a shoebox.**

This is where **you step in again.**

You notice that many of your customers, just like Jake, finish writing their songs but struggle with the mixing process. So you create a new product: a mixing guide, a template pack, or an EQ cheat sheet.

Jake buys it, follows your instructions, and **finally** gets his mix sounding professional.

Another victory!

But—surprise, surprise—**another problem appears.**

„WAIT… HOW DO I GET PEOPLE TO LISTEN TO THIS?"

Jake uploads his song to Spotify, expecting **thousands of streams.** He imagines waking up to messages from new fans, record labels knocking on his door, and an overnight success story.

The next morning, he checks his Spotify stats.

💀 **1 stream.** (And he's pretty sure that was him.)

Crap.

Now he's facing the next challenge: **music promotion.**

As an entrepreneur, you see this pattern. Musicians don't just need help writing songs, they need help marketing them.

So you create a music marketing course, a social media strategy guide, or a playlist pitching service.

Jake buys it, learns how to build an audience, promote his music, and actually **gets people to hear what he's worked so hard on.**

And just like that, he's hooked.

YOUR BUSINESS GROWS WHEN YOUR CUSTOMERS DO

Every time someone solves a problem, **a new one appears.** *"New level, new devil"* as I heard someone smarter than me once say on a podcast.

Jake's journey didn't stop after he wrote his first song. **Each step led to a new challenge.**

- Writing led to recording.
- Recording led to mixing.
- Mixing led to releasing.
- Releasing led to marketing.
- Marketing led to building a fanbase.

Every time he solved one problem, **a new one appeared.**

And that's exactly how **your business should grow.**

If you only sold Jake one product, you'd be leaving a lot of opportunity (*and money)* on the table. But by following his journey, anticipating his next struggle, and creating solutions for each stage, you don't just sell one thing. You create an entire ecosystem of products that keeps people coming back.

That's how you **keep creating new products**—by solving the **next** problem your audience faces.

It perfectly describes the **entrepreneurial journey** because as soon as your audience overcomes one challenge, **another one takes its place**.

This is why successful businesses don't just **sell one product** and call it a day. They **continue to create solutions** that help their audience progress to the next stage.

We can see how it plays out in a couple more industries below.

VISUAL ARTISTS & DESIGNERS: TURNING SKILLS INTO A BUSINESS

An aspiring digital artist **wants to improve their skills.**

- **Problem #1:** *How do I learn digital painting?*
- **Solution:** A step-by-step tutorial course on Procreate or Photoshop.

Once they **master the tools**, they now face a **new challenge**:

- **Problem #2:** *How do I develop my own unique art style?*
- **Solution:** A creative workbook with style exercises or a mentorship program.

Once they develop a unique style, they **want to monetize their art.**

- **Problem #3:** *How do I start selling my artwork?*
- **Solution:** A guide on setting up an Etsy shop, selling prints, or working with galleries.

Now that they're selling, their **next struggle** is growing their audience.

- **Problem #4:** *How do I market my art and attract collectors?*
- **Solution:** A social media strategy course for artists or a growth roadmap for Instagram and Pinterest.

Each solution leads to the **next level**, which brings its **own set of challenges.**

WRITERS & AUTHORS: FROM FIRST DRAFT TO FULL-TIME CAREER

A writer **wants to write a book.**

- **Problem #1:** *How do I start writing my first novel?*
- **Solution:** A novel-writing workbook or a „30-Day Writing Challenge" course. Trust me when I tell you that people buy this en masse, and I'm one of them.

Once they finish their first draft, they run into **a new obstacle**:

- **Problem #2:** *How do I edit and improve my book?*
- **Solution:** An editing checklist, self-editing course, or hiring an editor guide.

Now they have a polished book—but **what comes next?**

- **Problem #3:** *How do I publish my book?*
- **Solution:** A self-publishing masterclass or a step-by-step guide on getting a book deal.

Once they publish, they realize:

- **Problem #4:** *How do I sell my book and grow my audience?*
- **Solution:** A book marketing course, book launch strategy guide, or author branding toolkit.

Even **bestselling authors** constantly face **new levels, new devils**: book tours, foreign rights, audiobooks, film adaptations, and more. The **learning never stops.**

PHOTOGRAPHERS: FROM HOBBYIST TO PROFESSIONAL

A beginner photographer **wants to take better pictures.**

- **Problem #1:** *How do I use my camera properly?*
- **Solution:** A beginner photography course or camera settings cheat sheet.

Once they get comfortable with their camera, they **want to edit their photos.**

- **Problem #2:** *How do I edit photos like a pro?*
- **Solution:** A Lightroom or Photoshop editing course.

Now that their photos look amazing, they **want to start making money.**

- **Problem #3:** *How do I start booking clients or selling prints?*
- **Solution:** A business guide for photographers or a client contract template pack.

From there, they **run into even bigger challenges:**

- How do I price my work?
- How do I grow on Instagram?
- How do I start a photography business full-time?

Each step presents a **new challenge**, which in turn creates **new product opportunities.**

FINAL THOUGHTS: THE CYCLE NEVER ENDS

No matter what industry you're in, **problems don't disappear. They evolve.**

As your audience moves forward, they encounter new roadblocks. If you can anticipate those struggles and create solutions for them, you can keep serving the same audience at a higher level.

This is how successful businesses create **product ecosystems**—by guiding their customers through **each stage of their journey.**

The key takeaway?

- **Always be listening.** Pay attention to what your audience struggles with after they solve their first problem.
- **Stay one step ahead.** Create products that **help them move forward** so they keep coming back.
- **New level, new devil.** Once you solve one problem, another one appears. **That's not failure. It's growth.**

YOUR PRODUCT JOURNEY NEVER ENDS

Your first product won't be your **last.**

Think of your product journey like **learning to play bass.**

- At first, you just need to **know where the notes are.**
- Then, you learn **scales and runs.**
- Then, you move into **modes and advanced techniques.**
- Then, you work on **writing and playing increasingly difficult songs.**

Each step **builds on the last.**

(And remember: when I **lied about being a bass player** just to get a gig on tour, I had no idea what I was doing, but I quickly learned the basics by just playing **simple 1-5 Americana country bass lines.** It worked!)

Your business works the same way. Each product is just **one step** in your journey—both for you **and** your customers.

FINAL THOUGHTS: PUTTING IT ALL TOGETHER

Here's a quick recap of your **Three-Week Product Roadmap:**

WEEK 1: DEFINE YOUR PRODUCT IDEA & VALIDATE DEMAND

- Identify a **small, specific problem** to solve.

- Choose a **quick-to-create** product format (class, template, mini-course).
- Set up a **landing page** and drive **traffic** to test interest.

WEEK 2: ENGAGE YOUR AUDIENCE & BUILD YOUR OFFER

- Continue **posting content** about your topic.
- **Send emails** to build trust through storytelling.
- Create a **paid version** of your free product and build a **sales page**.

WEEK 3: LAUNCH, TEST, AND ITERATE

- **Launch** to your list and audience.
- Gather **feedback** and adjust as needed.
- Identify the **next problem** your audience needs help with.

This is how you build a sustainable business—by continuously solving problems, refining your products, and serving your audience in increasingly effective ways.

CHAPTER 7
SCALING UP AND CREATING MULTIPLE REVENUE STREAMS

HOW TO STACK PRODUCTS FOR LONG-TERM PROFITABILITY

Once you have successfully sold your first autopilot product, the next step is **scaling your income** by creating multiple revenue streams. Relying on a single product or service can be risky—diversification helps you build a more stable and profitable business.

Ways to expand your product suite:

- **Upsells & Bundles** - Offer additional resources or exclusive content to complement your main product.
- **Membership & Subscription Models** - Provide ongoing value with exclusive access to training, Q&A calls, or a private community.
- **Advanced Courses or High-Ticket Coaching** - Develop premium offerings for those who want deeper transformation.
- **Affiliate Partnerships** - Earn commissions by recommending complementary tools or services.

By stacking these revenue streams, you create a **scalable and sustainable** online business.

THE POWER OF COLLABORATION AND AFFILIATE MARKETING

Scaling isn't just about creating more products—it's also about **leveraging other people's audiences**. Strategic collaborations can help you reach a wider audience without spending a fortune on ads.

Effective Collaboration Strategies:

- **Guest Features** - Appear on industry podcasts, blogs, or YouTube channels to share your expertise.
- **Co-Branded Courses** - Partner with another expert to create a valuable joint offering.
- **Affiliate Programs** - Let influencers and content creators promote your product for a commission.
- **Joint Webinars** - Co-host events with other experts to introduce each other's audiences to your offers.

Building strategic partnerships **exponentially increases your reach and sales potential.**

WHEN TO AUTOMATE AND OUTSOURCE

As your business grows, it's crucial to **free up your time** by automating processes and outsourcing repetitive tasks. Doing everything manually will limit your ability to scale.

What to Automate:

- **Sales Funnels** – Use email sequences and evergreen webinars to sell on autopilot.
- **Customer Support** – Implement chatbots, automated email replies with FAQ sections for quick resolutions, and assistants to help you when it's taking you too much time.
- **Social Media Scheduling** – Use tools like Buffer or Later to batch content posting.

What to Outsource:

- **Graphic Design** – Hire freelancers to create visuals for your products and promotions.
- **Video Editing** – Have professionals edit course content, ads, or YouTube videos.
- **Admin & Technical Tasks** – Use virtual assistants to manage emails, bookkeeping, and scheduling.

By automating and outsourcing, you can focus on **big-picture growth strategies** rather than day-to-day tasks.

You've now built an autopilot business that generates revenue while you focus on creating more impact. In the final chapter, we'll discuss how to sustain this success, avoid burnout, and keep your business growing for years to come.

YOUR BUSINESS, YOUR RULES – THE LONG-TERM MINDSET FOR SUSTAINABLE SUCCESS

Building an autopilot business isn't just about making quick sales—it's about creating a long-term, sustainable income stream. To do this, you need to adopt a **growth mindset** and continuously refine your strategies.

Keys to long-term success:

- **Stay Adaptable** - Markets change, and so should your approach.
- **Keep Learning** - Stay ahead by continually upgrading your skills and knowledge.
- **Engage with Your Audience** - Build a loyal community that trusts you and your products.

A successful autopilot business doesn't just generate income. It allows you the freedom to work on projects you love while maintaining a balanced lifestyle.

AVOIDING BURNOUT WHILE GROWING YOUR BUSINESS

One of the biggest risks entrepreneurs face is burnout. When you're running a digital business, it's easy to fall into the trap of **constantly working**. To avoid exhaustion, you must set boundaries and create efficient workflows.

Tips to prevent burnout:

- **Time Blocking** - Set specific work hours and stick to them.
- **Prioritize Tasks** - Focus on high-impact activities and delegate the rest.
- **Take Breaks** - Step away from work regularly to recharge your creativity.
- **Automate Where Possible** - Use automation tools to handle repetitive tasks.

Success should not come at the cost of your health and well-being. Finding balance is crucial to sustaining your business over the long term.

YOUR NEXT STEPS: SCALING BEYOND YOUR FIRST SUCCESS

Now that your autopilot business is running, you may be wondering: **what's next?** Here's how you can continue scaling and refining your business:

Optimize Your Sales Funnels - Improve conversion rates by testing new messaging, offers, and email sequences.

Expand Your Product Line - Create additional products or premium upgrades to serve your audience further.

Build a Team - Consider hiring virtual assistants or specialists to help you manage growth.

Leverage Your Success - Teach others how to replicate your success through coaching or consulting.

Scaling isn't just about working harder—it's about **working smarter** and leveraging your existing momentum.

FINAL THOUGHTS

Congratulations! You now have a roadmap to building a profitable, sustainable autopilot business. The key takeaway is that you don't have to follow someone else's blueprint. You get to design a business that works for **you**.

Whether you're aiming for financial freedom, more creative expression, or simply more time to enjoy life, this business model gives you the flexibility to make it happen.

Now, it's time to **take action.** Apply what you've learned, stay committed, and build a business that supports the life you truly want.

And if you want some help getting there, check out the next page for an offer you might be interested in.

To your success,

READY TO TURN YOUR CREATIVE SKILLS INTO SCALABLE INCOME (WITHOUT FEELING LIKE A SLEAZY BRO MARKETER)?

If you've made it to the end of this book, you already know: marketing doesn't have to be sleazy, selling can feel like service, and your creativity *deserves to be profitable*.

I work privately with creative professionals—musicians, producers, writers, artists, and content creators—who are ready to turn their expertise into scalable digital income streams without burning out or becoming a content hamster on the Algorithm Wheel of Doom™.

This is high-touch, personalized support. No templates tossed over the wall. No "just watch this video series and figure it out." Here's a taste of what we might do together:

- Clarify your most profitable product or service idea
- Develop your signature offer or digital product (course, PDF, template, etc.)
- Map your customer journey and messaging so your audience actually buys
- Build or refine your marketing funnel and email automation

- Create a launch plan that fits your schedule, audience, and bandwidth
- Get personalized feedback on copy, content, and strategy—every step of the way

Every project is custom. Some clients work with me to launch their first digital product. Others build evergreen funnels for existing services. Some are done-for-you, some are coaching. What matters is *what works best for you and your goals*.

If you're serious about growing your business with more ease, clarity, and creative control—and you'd like expert help from someone who actually speaks your language—let's talk.

Reach out to me directly at **bjorgvin@bbenediktsson.com** Or apply here: **www.bbenediktsson.com**

Tell me a bit about where you're at, what you're building, and what kind of help you're looking for. If it's a fit, I'll send next steps.

This isn't open to everyone—I only take on a handful of private clients at a time to make sure each project gets my full attention (and no one's left screaming at a blank Mailchimp screen alone at 2am).

You don't need to have it all figured out. You just need to be ready to take the next step.

Talk soon,

THANK YOU (AND A QUICK ASK...)

Millions of books are published worldwide every year, so it feels like winning the lottery that you chose to read mine. I really hope that you enjoyed it, but more importantly, that it inspired you to make an impact with your own creative career.

Before you leave and put this advice into action, I'd love to know what you thought. If you enjoyed the book **please leave a review on Amazon (http://geni.us/rrevenue) or Goodreads to share your thoughts with others who may be interested in the book.** That's honestly one of the best ways to share these lessons with others that might benefit.

REMINDER: DON'T FORGET YOUR FREE GIFT

Before you leave and write a review on Amazon (that's what you were about to do right?), I wanted to remind you of the exclusive Rockstar Revenue bonuses you can access right here: https://www.bbenediktsson.com/rockstar-bonuses/

Here's what you'll get instant access to in the next two minutes:

- **Business Launch Checklist - Your Step-by-Step Startup Plan (Without the Headache):** Never started a business before? No problem. This simple checklist outlines everything you need to turn your business from idea to registered in your area, ready to sell to customers. No fluff. No legalese. Just the steps you need to go pro without losing your mind.

- **Go-To-Market Blueprint - Define Your Audience, Dial In Your Message, and Create Stuff People Actually Want:** If you've ever stared at a blank screen wondering who you're even making this for—this one's for you. This fill-in-the-blank workbook helps you identify your dream clients, clarify your offer, and test it fast (before you build a thing). Skip the overwhelm. Define your audience, message, and offer so you have a clear roadmap of what to do, and when to do it.

- **Creative's Pricing Calculator - Charge What You're Worth Without Guessing or Cringing:** This plug-

and-play calculator helps you figure out what to charge for your products or services—based on actual numbers, not vibes. Whether you're pricing a course, a sample pack, or a mixing job, this tool has your back. Knowing your numbers is everything. This calculator crunches the numbers for you, making it easy to know what to charge to maximize profit and shrink the timeline to your financial goals.

These high-value, high-impact bonus bundle is available to you for absolutely free for being a Rockstar Revenue reader. Simply go to https://www.bbenediktsson.com/rockstar-bonuses/ and grab them there.

Enjoy!
Björgvin

ACKNOWLEDGEMENTS

Over the last decade, I've had the privilege of speaking to students and creatives about online business and turning your skills into income. Thank you to every professor and program that invited me into your classrooms—you helped me shape the message that now lives in these pages. Your support was instrumental in helping me refine my message, hone my storytelling skills, and dial in the exact examples that gave people the inspiration to make an impact in their own careers.

To my wife, Liz: the valedictorian of my heart and the editor of my ego. You're my fiercest critic, my biggest fan, and the reason I still aim for straight-A material, even though the only grades I get now come from Amazon reviews.

To my marketing strategist, Anthony, who continues to be an instrumental brainstorming partner and an infinite source of perspective around marketing that keeps me pushing forward every day.

To my buddies in BLAMO: Chris, Lij, Matt, and Ian. It's absurd to think that I've woken up at 6 am every Friday for years just for the pleasure of your company, but your insight and support have made me a better human and a sharper entrepreneur. Here's for another decade of early morning Fridays!

To my my early readers and reviewers who helped me validate the contents of this book and help me see that it was worth publishing.

And finally, to every creative entrepreneur, musician, artist, and student I've worked with: thank you for trusting me to help you. Those "aha" moments you have—the ones where your eyes light up and you say, "Wait...I *can* actually do this?"—those are the moments that make this all worth it. You're the reason I keep writing, teaching, and showing up.

ABOUT THE AUTHOR

Björgvin Benediktsson is an Icelandic-American author, audio engineer, educator, and entrepreneur with nearly two decades of experience in the audio and online business industries.

He currently serves as an Entrepreneur-in-Residence at the McGuire Center for Entrepreneurship at the University of Arizona's Eller College of Management, and mentors early-stage startups at the UA Center for Innovation. In his career, he founded Audio Issues, an online education company serving thousands of customers worldwide, generating seven-figure revenue through digital products, courses, and software.

With a background in audio engineering, live sound, and musical performance, he bridges creative vision with business strategy. He has written for major industry publications, published best-selling books, and advises founders on customer discovery, digital marketing, and scalable revenue strategies.

His mission is simple: to help creatives and entrepreneurs turn their expertise into income – without selling out, burning out, or getting lost in the noise.